KISS AMERICA KISS

TrubuPRESS is a subsidiary of the Trubu Media Group whose interests include but are not limited to fiction and non fiction stories from the black experience throughout the American and African Diaspora.

Publisher: TrubuPRESS
Editor: Neo Blaqness
Cover Design: TrubuPRESS
Illustrations: Yolantha Harrison Pace
Proofreaders: Cynthia Utley, Tamika Coleman

Here's to Haiti: Kiss America Kiss
Copyright © 2013 Yolantha Harrison-Pace

All rights reserved. No part of this book may be reproduced or transmitted in any form or by any means without written permission from the author. Permission is granted for brief excerpts to be published for book reviews.

To order Here's to Haiti: Kiss America Kiss
visit http://trubupress.com
or call (872) 22TRUBU

Booksellers:
Retail discounts are available from TrubuPRESS. Inquiries about volume orders can be made via the phone number listed above.

ISBN-13: 978-0615886497
ISBN-10: 0615886493
Published by TrubuPRESS

PRINTED IN THE UNITED STATES

For my mother, Elaine...

Dear Reader,

Many of the things I see in Haiti are difficult for my heart to comprehend. I am not an artist, but in order not to cry and in order to pass the time when what I have witnessed keeps me from sleeping, I doodle. It helps to mend my broken heart.

This book is full of my doodles of love for Haiti.

Love you madly,
Yolantha

HERE'S TO HAITI
KISS AMERICA KISS

Story and Illustrations
by Yolantha Harrison-Pace

He's Got the Whole World in His Hands

WHO IS DEFINING WHOM

When I am in Haiti, the life culture is so extreme compared to what I see in America that it is hard to believe that someplace like America even exists. Surely then America is a fairy tale.

Then when I return to America, the life culture is so extreme compared to what I witnessed in Haiti that the nightmare I saw in Haiti surely cannot exist. I ask myself who is defining whom, for if I decided that there are no "wrong side of the tracks" and there are no "third world countries" or "wrong side of the ocean" perhaps then I could have the whole world in my hands.

HERE'S TO HAITI

A toast.

Here's to Haiti!

Children of a darker hue

Where children are what children do

When protected and connected

To the finer fruits of life

A Chablis abundant with love and joy

Roasts of peace and self control

Tall stemmed glasses of tenderness

Stew pots overflowing with

Faithfulness and kindness

Children will be what children see.

Here's to Haiti

A land undiluted by rose colored blindness

Yolantha...
You are not in Kansas anymore.

The brown blend
of earth skin
camouflaged the children
of the mountain
kids living abandoned,
naked and wild
no clue what it is
to be a child

A little boy blue is
Etched in my mind
A stunted little boy
In a gift blessed him
By an American missionary
A precious gift
Just the right big
To last him a lifetime

Two families of 18 people and 4 baby chicks live here.

HOMEMADE RECIPE

INGREDIENTS:

1 pair of well worn jeans

1 left behind missionary sheet

3 poles from by the wayside

5 large green banana leaves

DIRECTIONS:

Bind with love any way that you can

FRAME OF REFERENCE

"Hey missus!"

The naked teenager shouted.

"You know Whoopie Goldberg?"

I thought, how does a starving, naked teenaged boy on a remote mountain in Haiti know about Whoopie Goldberg?

I learned he had a cousin he visited one summer in Port au Prince before the earthquake who had a TV.

"Jumpin' Jack Flash" he shouted, "Jumpin Jack Flash!!!"

WHERE ARE WE

They stare at me

Their first black American ever

I am them

They are me

We are we

Looking at them I see

Chicago slums, 5th Ward of Houston

The ghetto of Harlem

I think

"There but for the Grace of God go I"

They stare at me

They think

"There with the Grace of God could we be"

HE CAN'T GO HOME

he can't go home without water
but all the wells are dry
he can't go home without water
but there's not a rain cloud in the sky
he can't go home without water
so again the village babies will die
he can't go home without water
so on his empty water bucket he sits
his eyes
too dry
to cry

THE NURSERY RHYME

He pumps and pumps and pumps.

Come on water come ooooon!!!

Too bad

too bad too bad.

All the water is gone.

He pumps and pumps and pumps.

Come on water come ooooon!!!

THE RIDDLE

I saw the smallest 10 carrots I'd ever seen in my life. I held 5 whole lemons in the palm of my hand.

"You know the difference between the Dominican Republic and Haiti?" the boy asked.

"No" I said, playing along with the riddle. "Tell me the difference between the Dominican Republic and Haiti."

"Fertilizer missus, fertilizer" He grinned real big.

For the life of me I could not find this funny.

Pretty girl with a stick

A pretty young girl by the side of the road.
There she sat. In her big wide straw hat.
Practicing writing with a stick.

By the road she sat
As still as still could be
Her fingers did sing
like hummingbird wings

What wasn't God thinking when women of color crossed His mind? A woman whose breasts nurtured nations; whose laughter tuned heaven with joyous vibrations.

A woman who with one bat of her eye, set men to war or soothed a baby's cry; whose spit could heal and take fake into the real; whose attentions could ostracize or bind.

What wasn't God thinking when women of color crossed His mind?

Generations take reservations just to linger on her lap. Upon her entrance the molecules change and adapt. Men try to own her, control her or even be her. When she's upset volcanoes her fire fear. She out-womans womanhood of every kind.

What wasn't God thinking when women of color crossed His mind?

THE LOOK HE GAVE

He proudly rode his mule
in the nude not to be rude
I asked what it felt like
to live in a third world country
the quizzical look he gave
put me to shame
"I don't know.
What is a third world country?"
That quizzical look was the same look
I remembered feeling when I was told
I lived on the "wrong side of the tracks"
My heart froze
realizing that in my Americanisms
I had just done to him
what had been done to me

THE MORAL OF THE STORY SO FAR

Wishes
Dreams
Hopes
Circumstances
Strategies

Wishes breed dependency on others.

Hopes and dreams come to fruition

When circumstances are met with strategies.

What I do…

There is rarely electricity so I work until the light is done. I work until there is no more sun.

Nobody knows the Haiti I've seen.

My white American Missionary companion sucked his teeth in disgust exclaiming, "As poor as they are, why in the world do the women keep having babies?"

MY HUSBAND IS DEAD

"Are you married?" I asked.

"No mam, my husband is dead."

Next home visit

"Are you married?" I asked.

"No mam, my husband is dead."

Next home visit

"Are you married?" I asked.

"No mam, my husband is dead."

I asked my translator was there a war, a disease that killed so many men?

"Men come and make many promises to the girls. You could call it a disease. They get what they want. The promises they do not keep. That is the epidemic."

Ah yes, I thought, the disease of empty promises. Black women and white women without abortion allowances have the same cancer in America.

THE GOD OF THE COOKIE

The household was so excited that I, "the Black woman from America" had come to their home. I gave the children a cookie so that we could visit. The mother and I talked about her family, their health and their education. I then gave her some food, clothing, tooth brushes, toothpaste, wide tooth combs, (the kind of combs Black people in America use) vitamins and aspirins that I had with me. At the end of our conversation I asked the mother if she had any specific prayer requests.

"Yes, I want to know your God of the cookies". All I could think was that my God is bigger than a mere cookie. But to the mother, the power of a cookie to silence her children for the length of our visit was a God worth knowing.

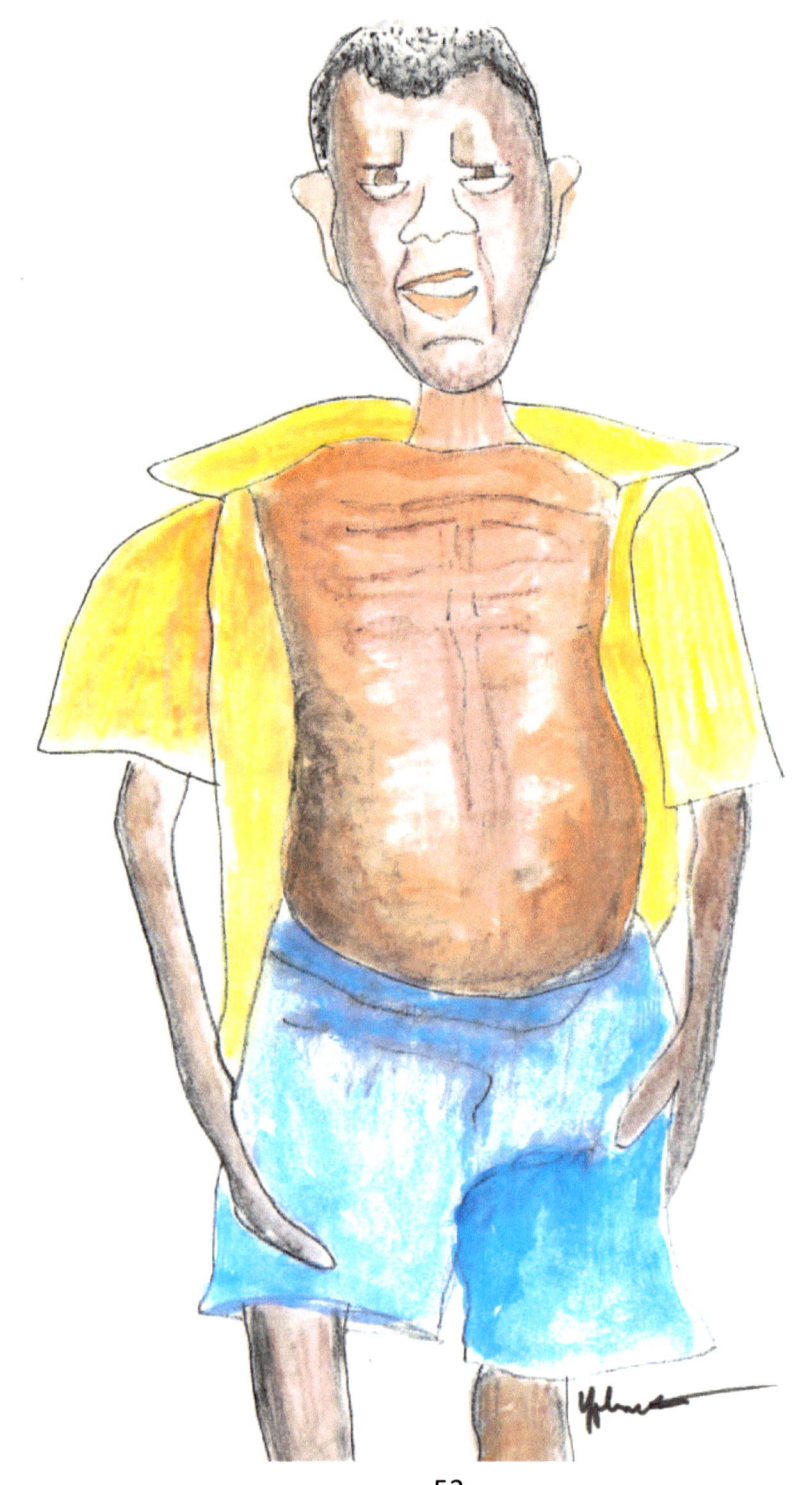

THE INTERVIEW

"What do you want to be when you grow up?"

"A person"

I giggled

"What kind of person?"

He leaned in real close to me as if I should have known the answer

"A good person"

"What would you like me to ask for or to tell the world if you could ask for or tell them anything?"

"Tell the world …

I am here."

WHAT IS CHEESE

"Do you go to school?"

"No missus."

"Why"

"We do not have money for the uniform"

"Do you want to go to school?"

"Oh yes missus"

"How old are you?"

"Twelve missus"

"What do you want to be when you grow up?"

"Oh missus, a doctor."

"May I take a picture with you?"

"Oh yes missus."

"Say cheeeeeeeeeeeeeeze"

She stands as close as close as close can be, leaning deeply into my motherness and says nothing. CLICK-FLASH goes the camera.

"Missus, what is cheeeeeeeeeze?"

A cloth of many uses.

They were all crowded into the classroom, ranging in age from two to 22 and had never ever seen a crayon. They knew of pencils and pens even though they didn't own them. But none of the children had ever seen a crayon, and when I taught them to cut paper with scissors they thought I was a magician or a wizard.

He tried and tried and tried to think.
"It has no lead, it has no ink."
He held the crayon between two fingers tight.
"What is her voodoo that makes it write?"

Jesus you said,
"Let the children come"
Well God, here they are.

FAST

"What are you doing big brother"

His sister asked

"I'm embarrassed, sick and

Ashamed of my past"

"But, but what are you doing big brother"

His sister asked

"the black woman from America

said pray to God

For a goodness that will last

You pray too little sister

For I'm praying that God will give us

All that he has"

"Okay, big brother, because we need God fast."

A school in America gave me backpacks to take to the children in Haiti. One American girl was sad she had no back pack to give so she gave me her jump rope it became the most perfect gift.

At school during recess the children had nothing to do so the next year I brought them a perfect gift too.

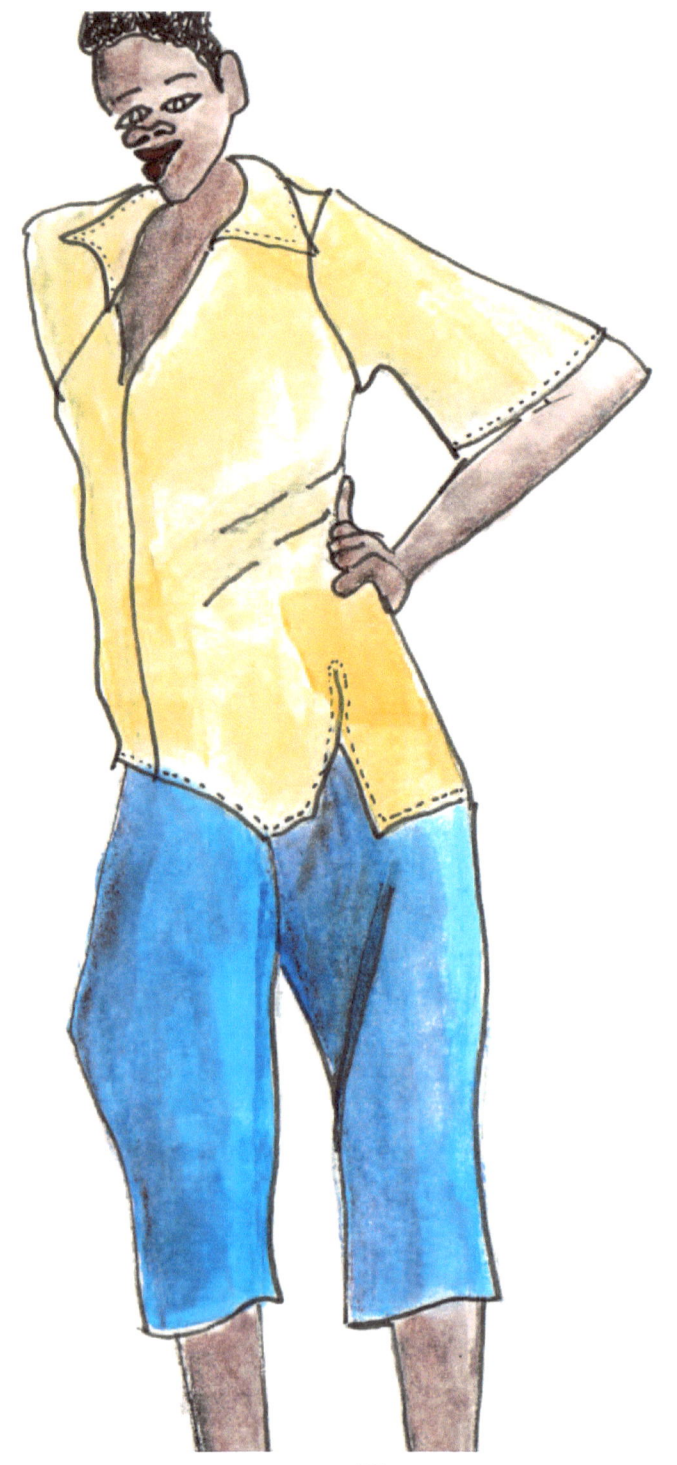

"Tell America thank you. Every night before we go to bed, my family prays for you Mix Youlanda and we ask God to bless America because you come. *(he looks to the sky and speaks louder)* GOD BLESS AMERICA.

Mix Youlanda, tell America thank you."

"Missus will you come again?
We will wait for you
Like the desert waits for rain."

BOBO, AMERICA, BOBO

Time to return to America.

A huge crowd of children chased after my truck.

As we picked up speed

Little by little

They all dropped off

Except one little future Olympian

He ran and ran his nakedness bouncing in protest

"Missus! Bobo America, bobo America!"

He ran and ran and ran and shouted and shouted

"Missus! Missus!

Bobo America, bobo!"

I turned to my translator.

"He is saying, 'missus, kiss America, kiss'"

The truck went faster, made a turn

And his voice

faded away in the wind.

www.ingramcontent.com/pod-product-compliance
Lightning Source LLC
Chambersburg PA
CBHW042007100426
42738CB00039B/31